WITHDRAWN

D1529235

EDGE BOOKS™

WARRIOR SCIENCE

MEDIEVAL KNIGHT Science

Armor, Weapons, and Siege Warfare

by Allison Lassieur

Consultant:
Josh Davis
Historian and Craftsman
Davis Reproductions
St. Paul, MN

CAPSTONE PRESS
a capstone imprint

Edge Books are published by Capstone Press,
1710 Roe Crest Drive, North Mankato, Minnesota 56003
www.mycapstone.com

Library of Congress Cataloging-in-Publication Data
Names: Lassieur, Allison, author.
Title: Medieval knight science : armor, weapons, and siege warfare / by Allison Lassieur.
Description: North Mankato, Minnesota: Capstone Press, [2017] | Series: Warrior science |
Includes bibliographical references and index. | Audience: 8–12. | Audience: 4 to 6.
Identifiers: LCCN 2015049408 (print) | LCCN 2016003006 (ebook) | ISBN
   9781491481301 (library binding) | ISBN 9781491481462 (eBook PDF)
Subjects: LCSH: Knights and knighthood—Juvenile literature.
Classification: LCC CR4513 .L37 2017 (print) | LCC CR4513 (ebook) | DDC 940.1—dc23
LC record available at http://lccn.loc.gov/2015049408

Summary: Describes the science behind the armor, weapons, training, and tactics
   used by medieval knights in combat.

Editorial Credits
Aaron Sautter, editor; Steve Mead, designer; Pam Mitsakos, media researcher;
Steve Walker, production specialist

Photo Credits
Alamy: Hilary Morgan, 13, Holmes Garden Photos, 15; Bridgeman Images: Biblioteca Nacional,
17, De Agostini Picture Library/G. Dagli Orti, 9, Look and Learn, 4–5; Dreamstime: Mikeaubry,
cover right; Getty Images: Dorling Kindersley, 28–29, duncan1890, 23, Heritage Images, 25;
iStockphoto: duncan1890, 20; Shutterstock: 3drenderings, cover bottom middle, 26 top right, 26
bottom left, 27 top right, 27 bottom left, conrado, 14–15, Dawid Lech, 19, Eky Studio, cover, design
element throughout book, Nejron, cover left, back cover, 6–7, optimarc , cover top, patrimonio
designs ltd, cover bottom right, Sibrikov Valery, 11, 16 left, 16 right, vadimmmus, cover bottom
left; Thinkstock: GuidoVrola, cover top middle

Printed and bound in China
PO007733LEOF16

TABLE OF CONTENTS

SCIENCE WON THE DAY

It was a chilly fall day on October 25, 1415, at Agincourt, France. Two armies grimly faced each other across a farmer's muddy field. An English army of about 6,000 men was gathered on one end. The English had already lost many soldiers to sickness. Those still standing were mainly archers and knights on foot. They faced a larger and stronger French army. The French had few archers. But the 20,000 French knights were ready to fight on horseback and on foot.

The English longbow was key to defeating the French at Agincourt in 1415. The powerful bows allowed the English to attack from a long distance to reduce the French forces and slow their progress.

As the Battle of Agincourt began, the heavily armored French knights sank into the mud. Wave after wave of English arrows rained down on them. The iron-tipped arrows pierced the French warriors' armor, using the force of gravity to kill. Hundreds of French knights fell and turned the mud red with blood. The French forces lost because of the weight of their own armor and the advanced science of the English longbow.

Knights were the European warriors of the **Middle Ages**. They often led armies into combat for land and power. The science behind their weapons and armor was often the difference between winning, or dying, in battle.

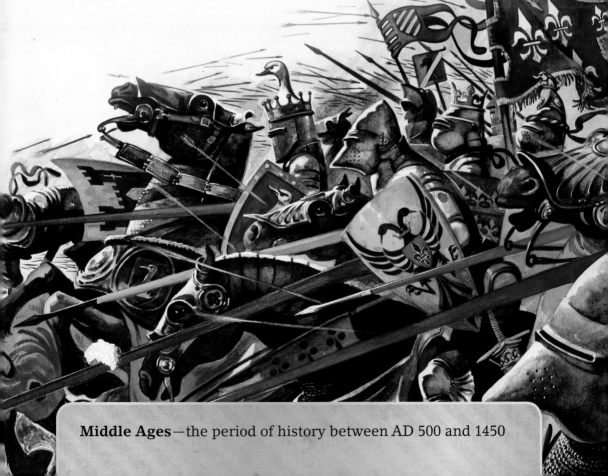

Middle Ages—the period of history between AD 500 and 1450

CHAPTER ONE

PROTECTION SCIENCE

From head to toe, a knight's armor was there for one reason—to keep him alive. To do that, a knight's armor used physics to his advantage. Physics is the science of motion, force, **momentum**, and energy.

Armored Protection

Every part of a knight's armor worked like modern bulletproof armor. Metal armor was thick enough to stop most weapons from puncturing, or going through it. It also didn't bend easily, which helped protect the knight from getting broken bones.

momentum—the amount of force in a moving object determined by the object's mass and speed

disperse—to spread out over a wide area

When a weapon hit the armor, it released energy. The armor worked to **disperse** and absorb the energy from the weapon blow. The armor spread the energy evenly across its metal surface, keeping the blow from injuring the knight.

Along with their strong armor, knights also used thick shields to block enemy attacks and absorb the energy of weapon blows.

Chain Mail

From about AD 1100 to 1300, knights commonly wore chain mail. This net-like armor was made from tens of thousands of small metal rings linked together. Bladed weapons couldn't cut through the tight mesh of metal links.

However, chain mail didn't absorb or disperse the energy from a weapon blow very well. It also bent easily. One good hit could result in broken bones and other serious injuries. It could also drive the small metal rings into the knight's skin. To protect against this, knights wore thick, padded tunics called *gambesons* under their chain mail. The gambeson helped absorb the energy of weapon blows during battle.

Gambesons and chain mail provided knights with a lot of protection. But this armor could weigh up to 50 pounds (22.7 kilograms), which could slow knights down during battle. However, the armor had good **weight distribution** which allowed the knight to be nimble in a fight. Even though the armor was heavy, it wasn't difficult to move around in.

FACT

It took several months to make one chain mail shirt. Only wealthy knights could afford one.

weight distribution—the way the weight of an object is spread out over a certain area

Chain mail was heavy, but it was very flexible. Some knights wore entire suits of chain mail for protection as they traveled.

Plate Armor

Over time knights gradually gave up chain mail in favor of plate armor. Every complete set, or harness, of plate armor was custom-made for the knight who wore it. The pieces were rounded and curved to fit the knight's body. The rounded shape of plate armor helped it to **deflect** sword and arrow attacks. It was difficult for enemies to get in a solid hit and do damage with their weapons. When weapons hit with a glancing blow, less force was transferred to the armor and the warrior.

Plate armor was often made with a fluting and corrugation design. This design used repeated bends and grooves to make plate armor more durable. It helped spread the energy of a weapon blow across many layers. This design is still used today to make sturdy cardboard and strong metal roofing.

In spite of its advantages, plate armor was very heavy and stiff. A full suit of plate armor could weigh between 60 and 80 pounds (27 and 36 kg). Plate armor badly affected a knight's mobility. Knights who fell in combat couldn't get up easily, which made them vulnerable to attacks.

deflect—to cause something to go in a different direction

DRESSED FOR BATTLE

HELMET
Helmets could weigh up to 14 pounds (6.4 kg). Most had rounded tops to deflect sword blows.

PAULDRONS
Pauldrons protected a knight's shoulders. They were made from several pieces of metal attached in layers. This design gave the knight full arm movement.

GAUNTLETS
The fingers and wrists of these gloves were made of several narrow metal layers. This design allowed a knight to fully grip his sword and swing it freely.

CUISSES AND GREAVES
Leg armor was especially important for a knight on horseback. His legs were often targets for armies on foot.

GORGET
This neck armor was usually made of two pieces of metal attached with a hinge and locked together. It overlapped the neck opening of the breastplate, so that swords and arrows couldn't get through.

BREASTPLATE
The thickest part of the breastplate was in the center and the left side. This helped absorb blows from a right-handed enemy.

VAMBRACES
These pieces protected a knight's forearms.

FAULD AND TASSET
These strips of hinged metal armor protected a knight's lower abdomen and hips.

CHAPTER TWO

THE SCIENCE OF BATTLE

The English weren't supposed to win at the Battle of Agincourt. But they had science on their side. They used the science behind their longbows to win the day. Throughout the Middle Ages, knights relied on the science of their weaponry to help them win in battle.

Deadly Swords

Killing enemies with a sword involved **velocity**, **mass**, and momentum. A knight used his strength and body mass to create force for a sword attack. With years of practice, a knight could deal a fast killing blow with a lot of momentum.

Knights used two basic types of swords in combat: arming swords and long swords. Arming swords were short, measuring about 2.5 feet (0.8 meters) long. They were good for speedy cutting or thrusting attacks. Two-handed long swords could be up to 4 feet (1.2 m) long. These were best for slicing and stabbing attacks. Their length also gave a knight the advantage of being outside of his enemy's reach.

 Most medieval swords weighed about 4 pounds (1.8 kg) or less. Their light weight allowed knights to strike fast and fight for long periods of time.

velocity—the speed and direction of a moving object

mass—the amount of material in an object

The Powerful Longbow

The English longbow was one of the deadliest weapons of the Middle Ages. Along with the bow's advanced design, archers often took advantage of gravity to make their arrows deadlier. They would shoot arrows high into the air so the arrows would accelerate while coming down. The increased speed gave the arrows greater **kinetic energy** to pierce armor and kill the target.

FACT

An arrow shot from a longbow could fly more than 720 feet (219 m). That's nearly as long as two and a half football fields.

1

English longbows were 5 to 6 feet (1.5 to 1.8 m) long. This length gave them a large **draw weight** of up to 180 pounds (81.6 kg). This large draw weight made them powerful weapons. It allowed the longbow to shoot arrows farther, faster, and deadlier than any other bow of the time.

2

English longbows were made of yew wood, which was strong, yet springy and flexible. It didn't take a lot of energy for an archer to draw the bowstring. The farther he pulled it back, the more **potential energy** was put into the string.

3

When the archer let go of the string, the potential energy was transferred to the arrow and became kinetic energy. This energy allowed the arrow to fly a great distance and pierce enemy armor.

kinetic energy—the energy of a moving object

draw weight—a measurement of how much strength it takes to pull a bowstring back

potential energy—energy stored in an object, waiting to be released

Heavy Weapons and Polearms

Knights didn't just use swords during hand-to-hand combat. They also fought with heavy weapons such as maces and flails. These weapons were strong and heavy, and were sometimes made with sharp spikes. These weapons could deliver more energy than a knight's armor could absorb. A well-placed blow could bash through a knight's heavy armor to injure or even kill him.

Some knights also fought with long polearm weapons. These weapons had various blades attached to long poles. Knights used them to attack enemies while staying out of range of most sword strikes.

flail

poleaxe

LOST SCIENCE OF AN ANCIENT WEAPON

During the Middle Ages armies in Europe were terrified of a mysterious chemical weapon known as Greek Fire. This destructive weapon was used mainly by the Byzantine Empire. The liquid fire was shot from metal tubes onto enemy ships, castles, and armies. It burned with intense heat and couldn't be put out with water. The recipe for Greek Fire was so secret that no single person knew all the ingredients. Even today no one knows the exact ingredients used to make Greek Fire. However, experts believe it was likely a mixture of petroleum, resin, and other flammable chemicals.

CHAPTER THREE

TRAINING WITH SCIENCE

Becoming a knight wasn't easy. Young boys started out as squires to older knights. Squires spent hours every day building their strength and learning the science of fighting.

Strength Training

Becoming physically strong was the first, most important part of a knight's training. Building strength started with progressive overload training. This process works by lifting a little more weight every day. The extra weight damages some muscle cells a little. The body then creates new muscle cells to fix the damaged area. This process results in stronger muscles and greater **endurance**.

Along with strength training, squires ran, jumped, and climbed walls while wearing armor. Each squire practiced jumping on and off a horse in full armor too. A future knight had to be able to ride and run long distances in his armor without getting out of breath.

endurance—the ability to keep doing an activity for long periods of time

quintain

Tournament Training

Squires practiced their fighting skills with heavy, wooden weapons. Sometimes they **sparred** with each other to improve their speed, accuracy, and aim. Other times, squires practiced these skills by hitting a large wooden post, or pell, for hours at a time.

Squires also learned balance, aim, and speed with long poles called lances. While holding a lance, the squire galloped on his horse toward a quintain. This device was a tall pole with a cross pole attached at the top to form a "T" shape. A shield or other target was hung on one end. Then a bag of sand or other weight was hung from the other end. When the squire hit the target, the pole spun around quickly. But the young knight had to keep moving. If he wasn't fast enough, the bag of sand could spin around and knock him off his horse.

FACT

Only one medieval quintain still exists in the world. Located in Kent, England, it is white with a pivoting bar on the top.

spar—to practice fighting

Waiting for the Right Moment

Medieval knights didn't fight by crashing their swords together like in the movies. That would have damaged a sword's sharp edges and made the weapon useless. There was only one way to win a sword fight in battle. A knight had to be the first to get his sword past his opponent's defenses.

To do this knights practiced kinesiology, or the science of human movement. The secret to staying alive in combat was simple—keep yourself and your weapon moving. A moving target was always harder to hit than one that was standing still.

A knight watched his opponent's movements closely to carefully time his attacks. When he moved in, he kept his feet spaced shoulder width apart for balance. He responded to the enemy's blows with counterattacks. A knight first used his strength and **body leverage** to deflect an opponent's sword strikes. When he saw an opening, he used his strength and body mass to thrust his sword into his enemy and end the fight.

body leverage—a motion in which a person uses his or her body like a lever to block an opponent and gain an advantage during a fight

CHAPTER FOUR

STORMING THE CASTLE

To protect their lands and people, kings and knights often built castles and towns surrounded by strong stone walls. These strongholds had to be captured to win a war. To do so, armies of knights relied on the science of **siege** warfare.

Siege Weapons

During a siege an army surrounded a city or a castle to cut off all supplies. However, a siege could last for weeks or months, depending on how many supplies were already inside. If the people inside refused to surrender, the knights would eventually bring out their battle machines. These special machines were built for one purpose—to destroy a stronghold's walls.

siege—a military blockade of a city to make it surrender

In the Siege of Acre in 1291, knights defended the walls of the city for 43 days before it was finally overrun by enemy forces.

Battering Ram

Knights often first tried to get past a castle's gate using battering rams. These large logs were suspended by ropes in a wooden frame. Soldiers first pulled the battering ram back and then let it smash into the castle gate. The swinging motion gave the ram momentum, which smashed into the gate with great force. Eventually the gate became weak and broke, allowing the knights to rush in. This method usually worked. If it didn't, it was time to bring in the big machines.

Mangonel

Mangonels had a strong arm with a bowl-shaped bucket that was filled with rocks. These weapons used the potential energy of a spring system to fling rocks and other objects through the air.

Trebuchet

Just one boulder hurled from a trebuchet could crumble a castle's wall. Trebuchets worked with the science of gravity. A long wooden arm had a sling attached to one end. A large rock or boulder was placed in the sling. The other end of the arm held a large **counterweight**.

When the counterweight was released, it quickly pulled the arm down. The arm in turn swung the sling through the air, which sent the rock flying. The heavier the counterweight was, the more energy it released to toss the rock farther and faster.

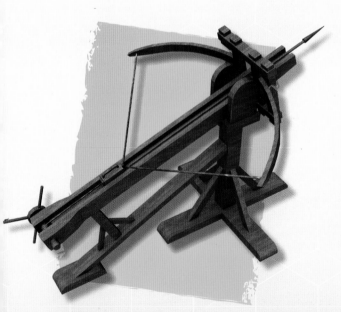

Ballista

This deadly machine looked and worked like a giant crossbow. It used the potential energy of a huge wooden bow piece to shoot large, heavy bolts at targets.

counterweight—the weight that balances a load

Mighty Fortress

The kings and knights who built castles knew how deadly siege machines could be. They used science to make their strongholds stronger and more difficult to attack.

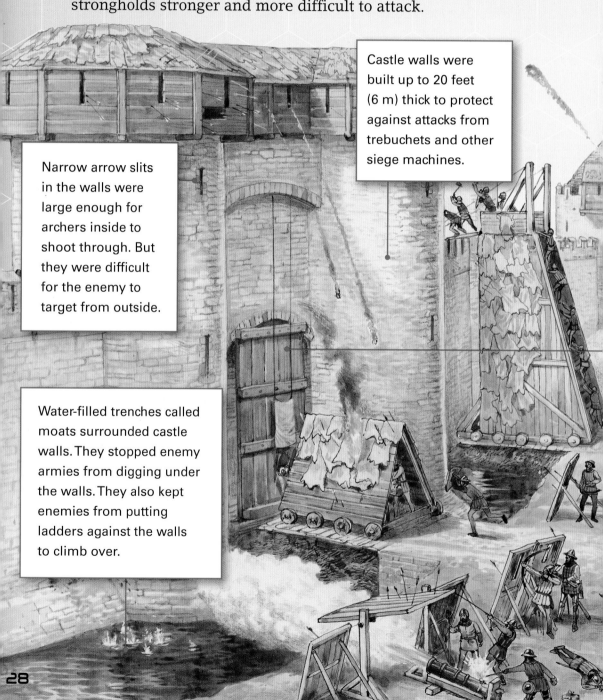

Castle walls were built up to 20 feet (6 m) thick to protect against attacks from trebuchets and other siege machines.

Narrow arrow slits in the walls were large enough for archers inside to shoot through. But they were difficult for the enemy to target from outside.

Water-filled trenches called moats surrounded castle walls. They stopped enemy armies from digging under the walls. They also kept enemies from putting ladders against the walls to climb over.

Science Kept Them Alive

Medieval knights often used science to their advantage. Science helped them make deadly weapons and protective armor. They relied on science in their training and battle tactics to find success in combat. Whenever a knight walked off a battlefield alive, he owed his life to science.

A heavy wood or metal gate, called a portcullis, hung from ropes and pulleys at the castle entrance. Pulleys help reduce the force needed to lift heavy objects. The pulleys allowed a single person to raise and lower the portcullis.

The geography of the land was used for extra protection. Castles were often built on a hill to get a better view of approaching armies. Hills also slowed down incoming armies.

body leverage (BOD-ee LEV-ur-uhj)—a motion in which a person uses his or her body like a lever to block an opponent and gain an advantage during a fight

counterweight (KAUN-tuhr-wayt)—the weight that balances a load

deflect (di-FLEKT)—to cause something to go in a different direction

disperse (dis-PURS)—to spread out over a wide area

draw weight (DRAW WATE)—a measurement of how much strength it takes to pull a bowstring back

endurance (en-DUR-enss)—the ability to keep doing an activity for long periods of time

kinetic energy (ki-NET-ik EN-ur-jee)—the energy of a moving object

mass (MASS)—the amount of material in an object

Middle Ages (MID-uhl AYJ-uhs)—the period of history between AD 500 and 1450

momentum (moh-MEN-tuhm)—the amount of force in a moving object determined by the object's mass and speed

potential energy (puh-TEN-shuhl EN-ur-jee)—energy stored in an object, waiting to be released

siege (SEEJ)—a military blockade of a city to make it surrender

spar (SPAR)—to practice fighting

velocity (vuh-LOSS-uh-tee)—the speed and direction of a moving object

weight distribution (WAYT dis-truh-BYOO-shuhn)—the way the weight of an object is spread out over a certain area

Critical Thinking Using the Common Core

1. If you were a knight, what kinds of armor and weapons would you use? How would that equipment help you win in a fight? (Integration of Knowledge and Ideas)

2. During a siege, armies on the outside used siege machines to invade a city or castle. Armies and citizens on the inside fought to keep them out. Do you think it would be easier to defend a stronghold or attack it? (Integration of Knowledge and Ideas)

Read More

Gravett, Christopher. *Knight.* DK Eyewitness Books. New York: DK Publishing, 2015.

Matthews, Rupert. *Weapons and Armor.* 100 Facts You Should Know. New York: Gareth Stevens Publishing, 2015.

O'Brian, Pliny. *Knights: Warriors of the Middle Ages.* History's Greatest Warriors. New York: Cavendish Square Publishing, 2015.

Internet Sites

FactHound offers a safe, fun way to find Internet sites related to this book. All of the sites on FactHound have been researched by our staff.

Here's all you do:
Visit *www.facthound.com*
Type in this code: 9781491481301

Check out projects, games and lots more at
www.capstonekids.com